# CONSTELLATIONS

# E. M. HANS

HODDER
Wayland

An imprint of Hodder Children's Books

*spinning through space*

# CONSTELLATIONS

Other titles in the series:  Comets and Asteroids •
• The Earth • The Moon • The Solar System •
• Space Mysteries • Space Travel • The Sun •

© 2000 White-Thomson Publishing Ltd

Produced for Hodder Wayland by
White-Thomson Publishing Ltd
2/3 St. Andrew's Place
Lewes
East Sussex
BN7 1UP

Editor: Sarah Doughty
Designer: Tim Mayer
Consultants: Teresa Chilton/Julia Hey,
Jodrell Bank Science Centre

The right of E.M Hans to be identified as the author of this Work
has been asserted by her in accordance with the Copyright,
Designs and Patents Act 1988.

A Catalogue record for this book is available from the British
Library.

ISBN 0 7502 2725 7

Printed and bound in Italy by G. Canale & C. S.p.A
Borgaro T.se (Turin)

Hodder Children's Books
a division of Hodder Headline Limited
338 Euston Road, London NW1 3BH

# CONTENTS

# THE NIGHT SKY

When you look up at the night sky on a clear, cloudless night, you will see the stars. They are suns, like our own Sun, but they are at least a million times further away from us. Away from the lights of a city, you will see the whole sky full of brilliant points of light. You might see a faint hazy pattern of light, called the Milky Way, making an arch overhead. You will feel that you can almost step out amongst the stars. Each one has a different name and place in space. If you want to find your way around the sky, you must learn the patterns the stars make.

The constellation map shows the following labels: Aquarius, Cetus, Pegasus, Aries, Eridanus, Delphinus, Andromeda, Triangulum, Pleiades, Taurus, Hyades, Cygnus, Cassiopeia, Perseus, Aquila, Lyra, Cephus, Orion, Serpens Cauda, Hercules, Ursa Minor, Auriga, Ophiucus, Draco, Gemini, Corona Borealis, Canis Minor, Serpens Capui, Ursa Major, Boötes, Leo, Hydra, Libra, Virgo.

▲ Constellations are groups of stars that make patterns in the sky. These pictures are from the northern hemisphere.

Think of stars as dots in a puzzle and join them up to make a picture. These star pictures are called constellations. Many of the names of the constellations we use today come from the ancient Greeks. Dividing the stars into constellations helps us to locate different stars in the night sky.

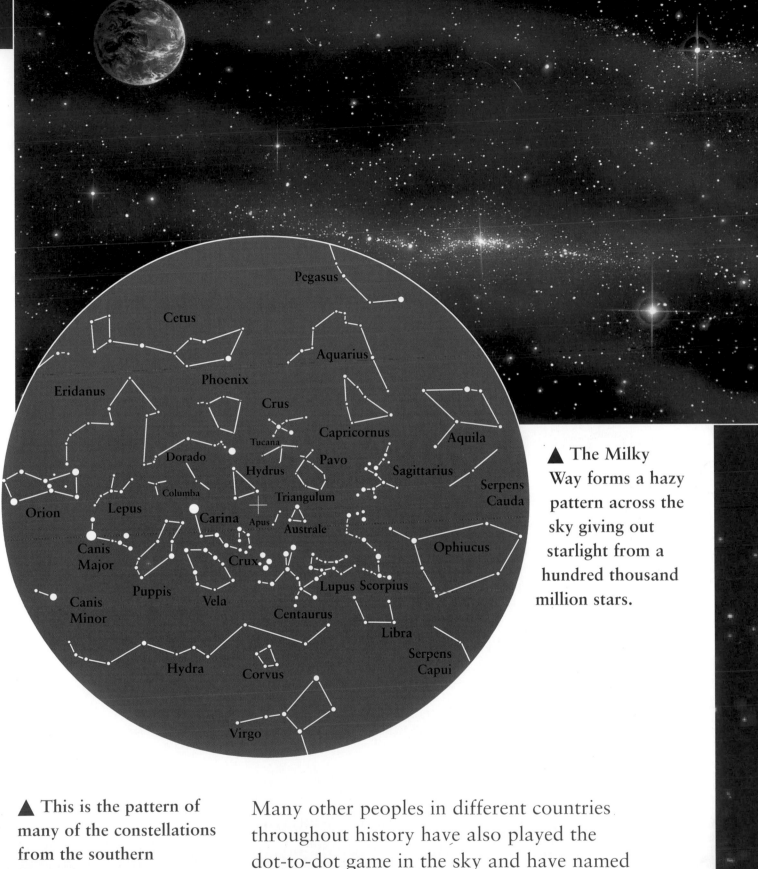

Pegasus

Cetus

Aquarius

Eridanus

Phoenix

Crus

Capricornus

Tucana

Aquila

Dorado

Pavo

Sagittarius

Serpens
Cauda

Hydrus

Columba

Triangulum

Orion

Lepus

Carina

Apus

Australe

Ophiucus

Canis
Major

Crux

Puppis

Vela

Lupus   Scorpius

Centaurus

Libra

Canis
Minor

Serpens
Capui

Hydra

Corvus

Virgo

▲ The Milky
Way forms a hazy
pattern across the
sky giving out
starlight from a
hundred thousand
million stars.

▲ This is the pattern of
many of the constellations
from the southern
hemisphere.

Many other peoples in different countries
throughout history have also played the
dot-to-dot game in the sky and have named
their own star pictures.

For people who live in different parts of the world, there are certain stars that are seen all year round. In the northern hemisphere they are called the northern circumpolar stars because they surround the North Pole. In the southern hemisphere, a different set of stars is seen around the South Pole, known as the southern circumpolar stars.

## The Great Bear

One of the best known star pictures in the northern sky is Ursa Major which means 'the Great Bear'. The seven stars of the Plough are part of the Great Bear. They are formed from the tail and hips of the Great Bear. Close to the Great Bear is her son, the Little Bear (Ursa Minor). This constellation is close to the position of the North Pole and includes the Pole Star.

According to Greek mythology, the Great Bear and Little Bear were thrown into the sky by their tails by the king of the gods, Zeus, to save them from hunters. Their tails were stretched so the bears have 'long tails'.

▲ Star pictures, such as the imaginary shape of the Great Bear, still guide us around the night sky.

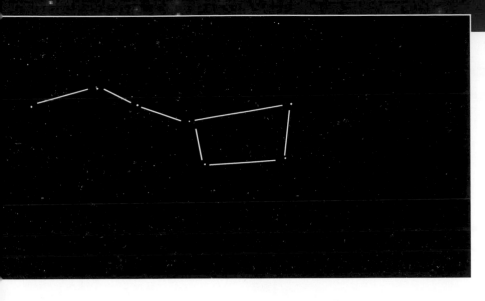

In Britain, these seven stars were thought to make up the shape of a plough.

Crux is the most famous constellation of the southern hemisphere – forming a clear cross in the sky.

The stars in a constellation are usually not near each other in space. They are just in the same direction as we see them from Earth. If we looked at the stars of the Great Bear (or Little Bear) from another part of the galaxy, they would make a completely different pattern.

## The southern skies

Many of the constellations seen in the northern hemisphere are also seen in the southern hemisphere in the same month of the year. But they are seen in a different part of the sky. The star patterns seen in the north are 'upside down' when viewed in the southern hemisphere. The circumpolar constellations of the southern hemisphere include Crux and Centaurus.

# THE SKY THROUGH THE SEASONS

The constellations seen in the skies are more easily visible in some months than others. To look at stars, you need to view them on a dark, clear night. Use the star maps on page 4-5 to help you find the positions of the constellations.

In the northern hemisphere the circumpolar constellations include Ursa Major and Ursa Minor.

## Northern spring/southern autumn

The constellations in the evening sky at this time of year include Leo the lion, Virgo the maiden and Corvus the crow. Leo is easy to find. Look out for a star shape like a question mark the wrong way round. This is the head and mane of Leo. Imagine the lion lying down with his front paws stretched out before him and his tail curled over his back. Behind Leo is a forked shape. This is Virgo the maiden. In Greek myth she is Persephone, the goddess of the spring. Close to Virgo is Corvus the crow.

▼ Some of the constellations visible in the northern spring and southern autumn.

Leo

Virgo

Corvus

| Northern hemisphere | | Southern hemisphere | |
| --- | --- | --- | --- |
| Northern spring | Leo<br>Virgo<br>Corvus<br>Hydra<br>Cancer<br>Boötes<br>Corona Borealis | Southern autumn | Leo<br>Virgo<br>Corvus<br>Hydra<br>Cancer<br>Vela |
| Northern summer | Cygnus<br>Lyra<br>Aquila<br>Delphinus<br>Hercules<br>Scorpius<br>Sagittarius<br>(Ophiucus) | Southern winter | Cygnus<br>Lyra<br>Aquila<br>Delphinus<br>Hercules<br>Scorpius<br>Sagittarius<br>Hydra<br>Boötes<br>Corona Borealis<br>Grus |

## Northern summer/southern winter

▼ Some of the constellations visible in the northern summer and southern winter. The individual stars Vega, Deneb and Altair are shown as star shapes in the illustrations below (left to right).

Northern skies are dominated by a bright triangle of stars called Vega, Deneb and Altair. Each one is in a different star picture, so if you find the 'summer triangle' you have located three more constellations. Vega is in a constellation called Lyra which represents a lyre, a musical instrument like a small harp. The star Deneb is the tail of Cygnus the swan and Altair is the bright star in Aquila the eagle.

Lyra　　　　　　　Cygnus　　　　　　　Aquila

| Northern hemisphere | | Southern hemisphere | |
|---|---|---|---|
| Northern autumn | Pegasus<br>Andromeda<br>Cetus<br>Perseus<br>Boötes<br>Corona Borealis<br>(Pisces)<br>(Aquarius) | Southern spring | Pegasus<br>Andromeda<br>Cetus<br>Grus<br>Piscis Austrinus<br>Capricornus<br>(Pisces)<br>(Aquarius) |
| Northern winter | Orion<br>Canis Major<br>Canis Minor<br>Taurus<br>Auriga<br>Gemini<br>(Lepus)<br>(part of Eridanus) | Southern summer | Orion<br>Canis Major<br>Canis Minor<br>Taurus<br>Auriga<br>Gemini<br>Perseus<br>Puppis<br>Lepus |

## Northern autumn/southern spring

Look out for the constellation of Andromeda. In Greek mythology, Andromeda was a princess rescued by Perseus from the sea monster, Cetus, who was turned to stone. Three of the stars of Pegasus and the end star of Andromeda make up the Square of Pegasus. This is easy to spot, as it is one of the biggest geometrical shapes in the night sky. Andromeda also contains the Great Spiral Galaxy.

▼ Some of the constellations visible in the northern autumn and southern spring.

Andromeda　　　　Cetus　　　　Pegasus

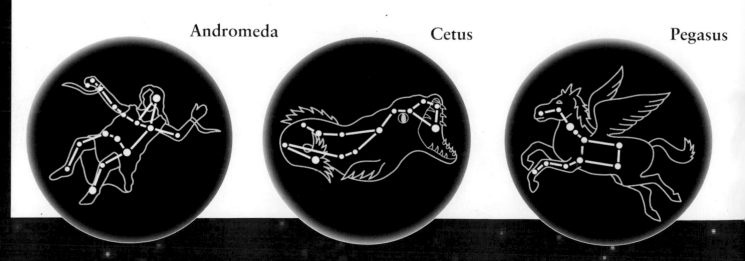

## Northern winter/southern summer

In the northern hemisphere, Orion, the hunter can be clearly seen. Look for three stars almost in a row. This is Orion's belt. There are two stars marking his shoulders and two more stars for his knees. Follow Orion's belt southwards away from this constellation and you will come to the brightest star in the night sky, Sirius the dog star. It is in Canis Major, the great dog. Making an equal-sided triangle with Sirius and Beltegeuse, (Orion's shoulder), is the star Procyon. Procyon is the brightest star in Canis Minor, the little dog. The star called Aldebaran is the eye of Taurus, the bull.

Orion's belt forms a distinctive part of this constellation.

▼ Some of the constellations visible in the northern winter and the southern summer. The individual stars Sirius, Procyon and Aldebaran are shown as star shapes (left to right).

Beltegeuse

Rigel

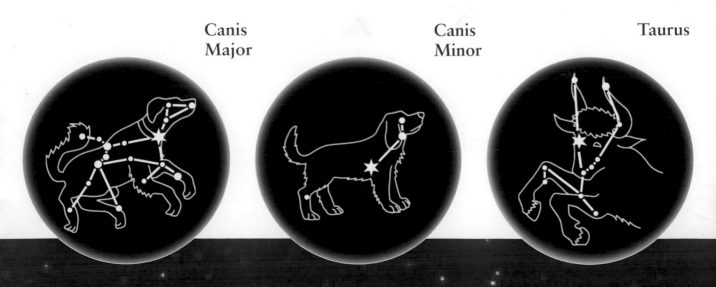

Canis
Major

Canis
Minor

Taurus

# DISTANCE TO THE STARS

The stars that make up constellations provide a pattern which help us to remember which star is which, but they do not tell us about the stars themselves. To learn what the stars are really like we have to look at them more closely. The most obvious thing about stars is that they have different brightnesses. However they are also at different distances from us. If we want to know how bright a star really is, we need to know how far away it is.

▼ Early astronomy in the observatory at Greenwich; one observer takes measurements while another uses a telescope to view the sky.

Proxima Centauri
The Sun

▲ Proxima Centauri is the nearest star to the Sun. It can only be viewed from the southern hemisphere using a telescope.

# Understanding parallax

To understand what parallax is, try this experiment. Cover your eye with your left hand. Now stretch out your right hand as far as you can, and with one finger block out an object on the other side of the room. Don't move the finger but change your left hand to the other eye. The finger will appear to have moved. This is because your point of view has changed. Do the same again but with your right hand nearer your face. The finger will appear to have moved even more. The amount the finger seems to move depends on how far it is away from your eyes. This is called parallax.

Hipparcos (190-120 BC) developed the method of trigonometry and used it to measure the lunar parallax, and so the distance from the Earth to the Moon.

In the same way, as the Earth moves around the Sun our viewpoint changes. Nearby stars will appear to change position against the background of more distant objects. This shift, called parallax, allows astronomers to work out how far away the stars really are.

13

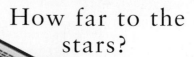

# How far to the stars?

The distances to stars are huge. So big, in fact, that we need a new way to measure them. We can measure distances on the Earth in kilometres. Distances between planets are in millions of kilometres, but the distances between stars are at least a million times bigger than that.

A convenient way of thinking about enormous distances is in terms of the length of time light would take to travel from one point to another. Light is the fastest thing in the Universe. It travels at about 300,000 km per second. That is about seven and a half times round the world in a second. It takes over eight minutes for light from the Sun to reach the Earth, which is 150 million km away.

▲ The satellite Hipparcos was the first satellite to produce an accurate map of the positions of over 100,000 selected stars in space.

A light year is a measure of distance, not time. One light year is the distance light travels in one year, roughly a distance of 9 million million km.

▲ The dog star, Sirius in Canis Major is the brightest star in the sky, 8.6 light years away.

Light from the 'nearby' star, Sirius takes over eight and a half years to travel through space to us. If you think about the difference between a minute and a year, it will give you an idea of how far away stars are.

A nearby star's distance can be calculated using the principle of parallax – measuring its position, twice, six months apart, when the Earth is positioned at opposite sides of the Sun.

When you look up at the night sky, the starlight you see has been travelling across space for thousands, even millions of years.

# FEATURES OF STARS

The radius of Beltegeuse is hundreds of times bigger than the Sun.

Once we know how far away a star is it is easy to work out how bright it really is. Some stars, like Sirius, look bright because they are relatively close to us.

Others, like Rigel in Orion, or Beltegeuse look bright because they truly are massive headlights in the sky.

▲ Beltegeuse is a massive red supergiant. It is the tenth brightest star in the sky, at least 5,000 times brighter than our Sun.

# Colours

Another difference between stars is their colours. If you look carefully at stars you should be able to see different colours. Some stars like Beltegeuse and Aldebaran are red. Arcturus is orange. Vega and Rigel are blue. Sirius and Altair are white and the Sun is yellow.

Their colour tells us how hot stars are at their surface. Red stars are the coolest at 3,000 °C. Yellow stars like the Sun are around 6,000 °C, white stars 10,000 °C and the hottest of all are the blue stars. Blue stars can be up to 20,000 °C and even hotter in extreme cases to over 30,000 °C.

By knowing how bright a star is and how hot it is, astronomers can work out how big it is. Very large stars, hundreds of times as big as the Sun, are called giants or supergiants. Small stars are called dwarfs. The Sun is a yellow dwarf.

Our Sun is a ball of hot gas 1.4 million km across. It is a yellow dwarf.

30,000+ °C
Hottest

Blue

Blue-white

White

Yellow-white

Yellow

Orange-red

Red

3,000 °C
Coolest

The blue supergiant Rigel, in Orion, is 140,000 times brighter than the Sun.

▶ Red stars such as Aldebaran are the coolest, while blue stars such as Rigel are the hottest.

# THE STORY OF A STAR

When we look at the sky carefully we see much more than just stars. There are also huge glowing clouds of gas and dust called nebulae, like the great nebula in the sword of Orion or the North America nebula in the constellation, Cygnus. These are really 'star factories'.

▼ Nebula in Orion. This is a starbirth region 1,500 light years from Earth.

**The birth of a star.**

Swirling nebulae of dust and gas are the birth of stars.

Gravity pulls the gas together and a spinning disc is formed.

Star spins and the dust and gas become flattened in a ring around the star.

Nuclear reactions begin with enormous energy.

Finally, the new star is formed.

# The birth of stars

The centre of a cloud begins to pull in the edges by the force of gravity so that the whole cloud shrinks down to form a spinning disc. As it does so, it becomes hotter. A star begins to form, taking up most of the material. Around it, planets and moons are formed by the rest of the gas and dust.

The first stars were probably formed over 12 thousand million years ago when the Universe came into being.

As the star grows, pulling in more and more gas, it eventually gets so hot and so squashed in the centre that a nuclear reaction starts and the star begins to shine. When that happens it blows away almost all the rest of the gas and dust around it.

Stars give out a lot of energy as light and heat.

# The death of stars

▼ This is a dying star in nebula Lyra. The white dwarf in the centre has blown its outer layers into space.

Within a large star, there is a battle between gravity and the outward pressure of heat. As hydrogen runs low in the core, the star sheds layers of gas. Eventually the core collapses. This can take the form of a tremendous explosion called a supernova which tears through the star and it dies. The death of a star is one of the most spectacular events of the Universe.

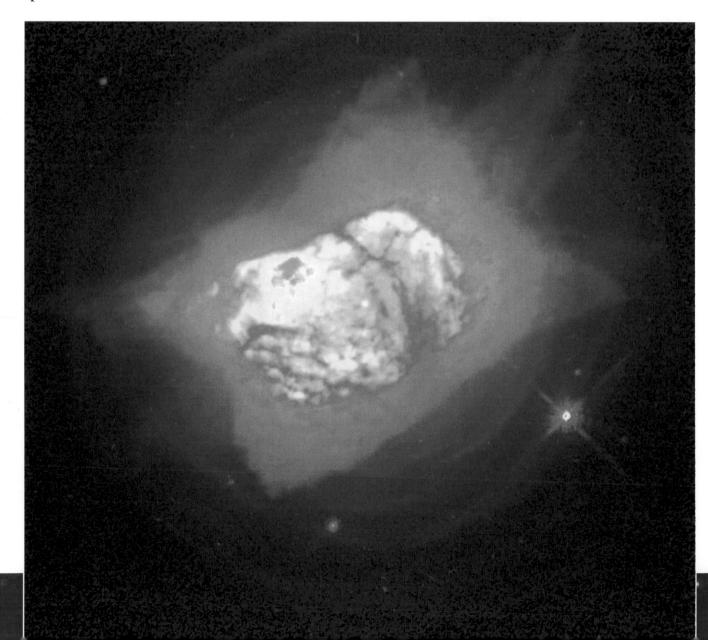

▲ This is how an artist imagines an exploding supernova would look.

## Dying Sun

Smaller stars like the Sun reach their end less dramatically. The Sun was formed over five thousand million years ago. In another five thousand million years the Sun will have used up all the hydrogen gas that it uses as nuclear fuel in its core. It will expand to engulf the planets Mercury and Venus and probably the Earth, too. Finally it will puff off its outer layers and shrink down to become a very hot dense star called a white dwarf, which will slowly cool over millions and millions of years.

All the debris left after the death of the Sun, including everything that is left of the Earth, will be recycled into the next generation of stars and planets.

# GROUPS OF STARS

A nebula often produces more than one star. Stars which orbit around each other are called double or multiple stars and are very common. In fact it is single stars like the Sun which are scarce. Most of the stars you can see in the night sky are double or multiple. Both Sirius and Procyon have white dwarf stars orbiting around them.

Some years ago it was suggested that the Sun had a companion star called Nemesis but it has never been found.

Double stars are held together by gravity. It is difficult to tell these stars apart without using a powerful telescope.

▼ The Alpha Centauri double star. These stars orbit each other every eighty years.

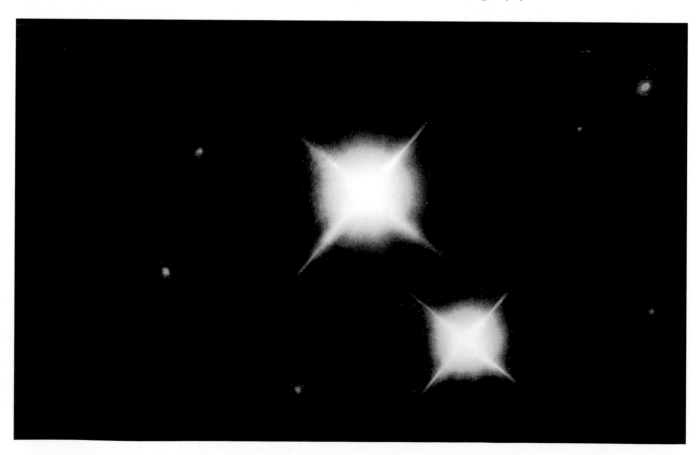

**▲ The star Mizar and its companion, Alcor.**

The star Mizar in the Plough travels though space with a much fainter companion, Alcor, that is close by. If you look through a small telescope you will see that Mizar itself is a double star.

Albireo, the eye of Cygnus (see Cygnus the swan on page 9), is a particularly beautiful double star because one star is sapphire blue while the other is golden yellow. The star Castor in the constellation of Gemini is multiple. What we see as one star is actually at least six stars, all orbiting around each other in a complicated gravitational dance. Life on a planet in such a system would be very interesting with six suns in the sky!

Astronomers study the orbit of double (binary) stars because this information can be used to work out the masses of the two stars.

# Star clusters

Very large nebulae can make whole clusters of stars. An easy cluster to spot is the Pleiades or Seven Sisters in the constellation of Taurus, the bull. If you look at the Seven Sisters on a clear moonless night you should be able to see six bright stars. With binoculars or a small telescope you will see dozens of 'sisters'. The very largest telescopes can show about 500 stars.

▼ The Pleiades, or Seven Sisters cluster. The cluster contains young, blue stars.

▲ Omega Centauri in the constellation Centaurus is the brightest globular cluster in the galaxy.

Globular clusters can contain a million stars.

There is another cluster in Taurus which is also easy to see. The stars that make up the V-shape of the bull's head (see page 11) are part of a cluster called the Hyades. The star Aldebaran, the bull's eye, is not part of the Hyades. It is roughly half way between us and the cluster. You can tell that the Hyades are closer to us than the Seven Sisters because the Hyades cluster looks bigger in the sky than the Seven Sisters and the stars appear to be further apart.

## Globular clusters

The Hyades and Pleiades are called open clusters. They are made up of bright, young stars. But there is another type of star cluster. It is called a globular cluster. Globular clusters contain some of the oldest stars in the Milky Way. They are found round the outside of our galaxy.

# GALAXIES

## The Milky Way

All the stars, clusters and nebulae we have been looking at so far are part of our galaxy, the Milky Way. Seen edge on, the Milky Way is a flat disc shape with a bulge of stars in the middle called the nucleus. The globular clusters are scattered in a sphere around the disc. This is called the halo of the galaxy.

The solar system revolves around the middle of the Milky Way about once every 225 million years.

▼ The Earth is part of the solar system which is part of the Milky Way which is part of a bigger cluster of galaxies.

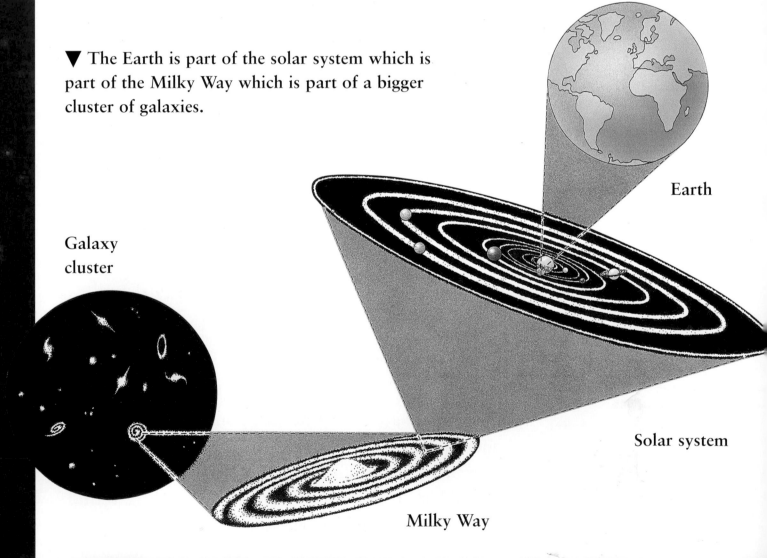

Galaxy cluster

Earth

Solar system

Milky Way

▲ Our Milky Way
measures approximately
100,000 light years across.

The disc is where the open clusters, nebulae and
most of the stars, particularly the youngest ones,
are found. They are not spread out evenly on the
disc. Rather they make a sort of spiral pattern
like a Catherine Wheel or a whirlpool. The solar
system is not in the centre of the galaxy. It is in
one of the spiral arms two-thirds of the way
from the centre out towards the edge of
the disc. The centre of the Milky Way
lies in the direction of the constellation
of Sagittarius, the archer. We cannot see
the centre because there is so much gas
and dust in the way. All the stars, gas and
dust orbit around the centre of the Milky Way,
just as the planets orbit the Sun.

The
constellation Sagittarius
contains more stars than any other
constellation because the centre of
the galaxy lies in that direction.

▶ Spiral galaxies have a bright centre with arms of stars curving out in a spiral shape.

The Milky Way has two small galaxies orbiting around it. They are called the Magellanic clouds.

▼ Elliptical galaxies vary in shape from circular to oval.

## More galaxies

When we use a large telescope to look beyond the stars of the Milky Way, we can see many other galaxies. They come in different shapes and sizes. Many are ordinary spiral galaxies like the Milky Way. Some are barred spirals, where the spiral arms start from a bar of stars extending on either side of the nucleus. Others are elliptical. They may be small, or huge with hundreds of times as many stars as the Milky Way. Some galaxies have no particular shape. These are described as irregular.

▶ Irregular galaxies are often smaller than elliptical or spiral galaxies and do not have a well-defined structure.

◀ The Great Spiral Galaxy in Andromeda and the Milky Way are part of a cluster of galaxies called the Local Group.

## Across the Universe

The closest large galaxy to the Milky Way is the Andromeda galaxy. It can only just be seen without a telescope. It looks like a faint hazy patch on the sky. Galaxies form larger groups, called clusters. The Milky Way and the Andromeda galaxy are part of a cluster called the Local Group, which stretches three million light years across space and forms part of an even larger supercluster. This is just one of many other superclusters stretching for many millions of light years across the Universe.

The Andromeda galaxy is approximately 2.9 million light years away as measured by the Hipparcos satellite.

# GLOSSARY

**Astronomers** People who study the science of the Universe.

**Binary stars** Two stars that revolve around each other, locked in together by gravity.

**Circumpolar** The stars that revolve around the poles, and do not set.

**Clusters** Groups of stars or galaxies that lie close to each other.

**Dwarf star** An ordinary star like the Sun, or a very small old star.

**Elliptical** Shaped like a flattened circle.

**Galaxy** A massive group of stars, dust and gas, drawn together by gravity.

**Globular cluster** A group of a few thousand to a million stars that are found in the 'halo' of our galaxy.

**Gravity** A force of attraction between two objects.

**Hemisphere** Half of a sphere, such as the northern or southern part of the Earth.

**Hydrogen** An invisible gas, with no colour or smell.

**Light year** The distance that a ray of light travels in a year; over 9 million million km.

**Lunar** To do with the Moon.

**Mass** The amount of matter in an object, measured in kilograms.

**Milky Way** A broad band of light in the sky created by the millions of stars that make up our galaxy.

**Nebula** A cloud of gas or dust in space.

**Nuclear reaction** When atoms of gas in a star join together to make large atoms, creating heat and light.

**Nucleus** Refers to the centre of an object, such the dense part in the middle of a galaxy.

**Radiation** The waves of energy, heat or particles from an object.

**Trigonometry** The part of maths that is to do with the relationship between the sides and angles of a triangle.

# FURTHER INFORMATION

## Web pages:

http://windows.engin.umich.edu/the_universe/
Constellations/constnavi.html
Constellations in the northern and southern hemispheres; sky maps; myths; suitable from beginner to advanced.
http://www.emufarm.org/~cmbell/myth/myth.html
The mythology of the constellations.

## Books to read:

*Beyond the Night Sky* by Chris Oxlade (Collins Trailblazers, 1996)
*The Children's Space Atlas* by Robin Kerrod (Apple Kids, 1991)
*Guide to Space* by Peter Bond (Dorling Kindersley, 1999)
*Let's Look at the Sky* by Donald Grant (Moonlight Books, 1999)

*Looking into Space* by Nigel Nelson and Piers Harper (Readers Digest Children's Books, 1998)
*The Usborne Complete Book of Astronomy and Space* by Lisa Miles and Alistair Smith (Usborne, 1998)

## Places to visit:

Jodrell Bank Science Centre, Macclesfield, Cheshire, SK11 9DL (Tel: 01477 571339)
The Planetarium, Euston Road, London (Tel: 0207 935 6861) has shows which feature stars and planets.
The Science Museum, Exhibition Road, South Kensington, London (Tel: 0207 938 8000) includes lots of astronomy exhibits.
The Royal Observatory Greenwich, London (Tel: 0208 312 6557) includes historical telescopes and has a planetarium.

## CONSTELLATIONS

**SCIENCE**
- Using planispheres (moveable star maps) study the night sky.
- Experiment with parallax.

**HISTORY**
- Research the myths and legends of Greek mythology: Orion, Perseus, Pegasus, Andromeda, Cassiopeia, etc.
- Find out about famous Greek astronomers such as Ptolemy.

**GEOGRAPHY**
- Describe the position of the constellations using directionals (north, south etc).

**DESIGN AND TECHNOLOGY**
- Make a 3D map of the sky using papier mâché over a balloon. Paint it black and add the stars.

**ART AND CRAFT**
- Draw your own figures for constellations. Choose some of the lesser known ones and use your imagination to see the star picture.

**ENGLISH**
- Describe an imaginary journey to a different galaxy.

**MATHS**
- Represent data of the skies (e.g. star distance, brightness), graphically.

# INDEX

All numbers in **bold** refer to pictures as well as text.

**Picture acknowledgements:**
The publishers would like to thank the following for allowing their pictures to be reproduced in this book: Bruce Coleman/Astrofoto 6; Eye Ubiquitous cover (inset top); Mary Evans Picture Library title page; Genesis 14; HWPL 7 (both), 12; Science Photo Library 18, 22/Celestial Image Picture Company cover (inset middle), 29,/Julian Baum 13,/Chris Butler 27,/John Chumack 16,/Luke Dodd 25,/David Ducros 5,/David A. Hardy 28,/Mehau Kulyk 21,/Pekka Parviainen 23,/Ronald Rover cover (main), 24,/John Sanford 15,/Robin Scagell 11,/Space Telescope Science Institute/NASA 20 and cover (inset bottom). Artwork by Peter Bull Art Studio except page 26 (HWPL).